Original title:
The Shelter of a House

Copyright © 2025 Creative Arts Management OÜ
All rights reserved.

Author: Beckett Sinclair
ISBN HARDBACK: 978-1-80587-072-2
ISBN PAPERBACK: 978-1-80587-542-0

Moments Between the Doorways

In the hallway where socks go to hide,
I trip on the dog's tail, takes me for a ride.
The cat gives a glare, like I'm breaking a rule,
While I'm juggling my snacks, feeling quite the fool.

The kitchen's a circus, pots dance in a line,
Spaghetti's a noodle, so messy yet fine.
Mom's recipe calls for a pinch of pure luck,
As flour clouds flutter, oh what a muck!

The living room's chaos, pillows soaring high,
Each toss turns a couch into clouds in the sky.
Siblings are giggling, dodging a throw,
As a blanket fort rises, just watch it grow!

Between the bright frames, memories collide,
Wobbling through laughter, we take it in stride.
Every moment's a treasure, no need to be grand,
In corners and nooks, life's fun is well planned.

Comforting Corners

In corners tight where dust bunnies play,
The cat holds court, ruling the day.
Old socks and toys, quite the display,
A fortress of comfort, come what may.

The couch leans in, a soft, warm hug,
Its cushions filled with each lost mug.
We laugh at the mess, quite the snug tug,
In comforting corners, we're all just a rug.

The Spirit Within

Come find your spirit, it's hiding well,
Under the stairs, where old stories dwell.
With squeaky floors and a forgotten bell,
A ghost of giggles, ready to tell.

It dances through halls, a whimsical breeze,
Tickling the curtains, shaking the leaves.
With mischief and magic, it never leaves,
A home's heart whispers, and laughter weaves.

Reflections of Love

Mirrors in hallways, catching our dreams,
Where each glance reflects our shared schemes.
In family photos, the laughter redeems,
A tapestry woven with silly themes.

Crumbs on the counter, a snack of delight,
Shared pizza and jokes, a cozy night.
As memories twinkle, oh, what a sight,
Together we shine, our joy taking flight.

Resilience in Rooflines

Raindrops tap dance on shingles above,
While laughter echoes, as warm as a hug.
The roof stands strong, a guardian of love,
Protecting our moments, like a snug bug.

With each crack and creak, we turn to embrace,
The stories that linger, their silly trace.
In resilience found, we harness our space,
With hearts as our anchors, we dash in the race.

Kindling Kindness

In the corner, a cat on a chair,
Snoozing softly without a care.
The old dog dreams of chasing a cat,
While the goldfish swims in a funky hat.

Jars of pickles line the shelf,
With one that claims to heal oneself.
Grandma's stew simmers with flair,
Leaving us laughing in the thick of air.

A Haven of Echoes

The clock ticks loud, a comical chime,
Telling tales of the silliest time.
Mom's slippers squeak like a mouse,
As she dances around the house.

The mirrors giggle, reflecting our glee,
Each glance revealing a sight to see.
Styles from the past, like awful hair,
Make us chuckle without a care.

Gables of Grace

The roof is lopsided, quite a mess,
But it still holds the hundredth guess.
Rain trickles down like a leaky tap,
Creating puddles for a splashy snap.

Windows rattle with jokes of old,
Stories of sequins once made of gold.
A family portrait that's slightly askew,
Shows our best side, or maybe just a few!

Hearth of the Heart

By the fire, marshmallows sing,
While socks wander off, what a fling!
Popcorn pops with a joyful cheer,
Bouncing around, oh what a year!

Chairs do tango, the floors creak and sway,
While we laugh like children at the end of the day.
In this cozy mess where warmth abides,
Laughter's the weather, and love never hides.

Cradled in Connection

Inside these walls, we laugh and play,
Where socks are lost, and pets delay.
A kitchen dance, a breakfast fight,
Who knew toast could take such flight?

Family meetings, all at once,
Discussing who's the silliest dunce.
The dog barks loud, the cat retreats,
We make our plans over messy treats.

The Gate to Serenity

A squeaky door with tales to tell,
Of neighbors' gossip and cookie smell.
We peek outside, what do we see?
A squirrel plotting a heist with glee.

The garden's wild, weeds out of hand,
Yet blooms still rise, and all is grand.
Tomato plants may flop and droop,
But who can frown while dodging poop?

Resilience of Roofs

When storms blow hard, we brace our backs,
Old tiles rattle, there's no relax.
Yet laughter spills through thunder's roar,
As we declare our games galore!

Fortress strong, with faded paint,
We sing off-key, a joyful taint.
A roof that leaks is not so bad,
When life's a laugh, it makes us glad.

Comfort in the Chaos

Pillows piled, a mountain high,
We tumble in, then start to fly.
The TV's loud, the kids are wild,
Yet peace arrives when chaos smiled.

Dishes stacked like a giant tower,
We make a game, it's our power.
Amidst the mess, we find our way,
Together here's where we will stay.

Cracks in the Ceiling

Up on the ceiling, a crack has spread,
It looks like a map of where dreams once bled.
I swear I saw a squirrel making its nest,
Singing to the cracks, thinking it's best.

With each little tremor, it starts to dance,
A jig to the tune of a homey romance.
I laugh at the shadows that twist and twirl,
Who knew a crack could result in a whirl?

Heart's Resting Place

In the corner sits a chair, quite proud,
With pillows that giggle, they're always loud.
They cushion my thoughts, hold all my dreams,
Whispering secrets in soft, fluffy schemes.

The coffee pot's always in charge of the fun,
Brewing hot gossip under the sun.
A place where my worries can take off their shoes,
And dance around freely, picking and choosing.

Nest of Narratives

In the corner of rooms, tales rise like steam,
Poking each other like a kid's wild dream.
An old shoe shines with adventures untold,
Socks plotting heists, daring and bold.

With each quirky item, stories unfold,
A goldfish once lived on skirts made of gold.
It's a gathering place for forgotten lore,
Where knickknacks chatter and laughter does soar.

Walls That Tell Stories

The walls creak and croak, like an old-time bard,
They tell funny tales, a little bit weird.
From the time I spilled juice at a family feast,
To the wall that ate cupcakes—not one, but at least!

Each dent has a punchline, a witty refrain,
A battle with furniture, me, sprained in pain.
So here's to the walls, keepers of cheer,
With their silly old secrets, we hold oh so dear.

Twilight in the Hallway

In the dim light, a sock does hide,
Wandering cats know where they bide.
A shoe with a story, lost and forlorn,
As dust bunnies plot, we all are worn.

The fridge hums songs, a tune so sweet,
While leftovers dance, a spontaneous treat.
Mismatched chairs hold our tales of cheer,
In this cozy nook, there's nothing to fear.

Shadows of Familiarity

In the corners, shadows play peek-a-boo,
Familiar faces of furniture, too.
The lamp tells secrets of midnight snacks,
While dishes chuckle at our wild acts.

Old cushions groan under our generous weight,
Pillows gossip as we speculate fate.
Curtains sway with a playful tease,
Whispering laughter on a gentle breeze.

Hearthside Harmony

The fire crackles, a pop and a snap,
S'mores and stories in an awkward lap.
With marshmallow stuck to my favorite sock,
We'll toast to the night with a hearty mock.

A blanket fight breaks out with a laugh,
As dad's mismatched socks steal the craft.
Mom joins in with a feigned martial arts,
In this chaotic dance, happiness starts.

Embracing the Ordinary

Who knew a dustpan could bring such glee?
With each scoop of crumbs, a grand jubilee.
The broom does tango, sweeping in time,
While we conspire with laughter to rhyme.

In the mundane, a joke often found,
Where everyday antics seem quite profound.
We hide from the world in our quirky tune,
With echoes of laughter that chase the moon.

Refuge from the World

Inside these walls, I'm free to dream,
A fortress built on laughter's beam.
The laundry pile—its own mountain range,
Each sock a quest, a little strange.

The fridge hums tunes, a steady hum,
While I'm the king, and they're the crumbs.
Every chair's a throne, plush and wide,
As I reign over this comfy tide.

Whispers in the Attic

Lurking up high, the dust bunnies plan,
Plotting the chaos while I brew a can.
An old lamp flickers with secrets to tell,
While I serve popcorn to my fuzzy pals.

The shadows cast stories of long-lost toys,
Their giggles echo, those mischievous boys.
I'll join their adventure, a comical ride,
In the attic's embrace, we can bumble and glide.

Spirit of the Entryway

Welcome mats greet with cheeky grins,
As shoes gather tales of outside sins.
With every step, they squeak and squeal,
Oh, the drama here is all too real!

The coat rack's an octopus ready to strike,
Hats tangled in chaos, oh what a hike!
I trip over friendships, here on the floor,
Each fall an invitation for laughter galore.

Heartbeat of the Home

The oven hums songs of warm delight,
While pots and pans chime in the night.
"Dinner's ready!" I hear the call,
As my cat dives headfirst into the hall.

Stirring soup and secrets, the broth aligns,
Conversations simmer like hidden wines.
Here in this kitchen, the fun unfolds,
With each swirling pot, a new tale told.

Whispers of the Past

In the attic, old boxes lie,
A mouse scurries by, oh my!
Dust bunnies doing a jig,
While Grandma's hat fits like a twig.

Photos faded, smiles askew,
Uncle Joe's dance moves, quite the view.
A coat rack sings stories of yore,
As shoes and boots trip on the floor.

Chairs creak with tales, bold and bright,
While the fridge hums softly at night.
The closet sometimes seems to sigh,
When secrets escape with a laugh and a cry.

So here we gather, our hearts a tune,
Sharing ghosts with a laugh or a croon,
For every room has a tale to tell,
In this wacky haven, we all dwell.

An Ode to the Threshold

Oh what a fine place we pass through,
Where shoes pile high, and friends swoon too.
The doorbell rings, and chaos ignites,
As we tumble in, ready for bites!

The welcome mat says 'please come in,'
As socks go missing like they've taken a spin.
Squeaky hinges gossip our return,
While jackets dance, upon each turn.

A step on the mat with a joyful thud,
Makes the neighbors stare, thinking it's a flood.
Welcome to chaos, and laughter's embrace,
Where everyone trips, but none lose their grace.

So let's adore this threshold divine,
Where every footstep feels like a sign.
Here's to the hugs and the shouts that fly,
This entryway's magic, oh me, oh my!

Making Memories on the Stairs

On the stairs we tumble and slide,
Eager to see what secrets hide.
Each step creaks a comical song,
As tiny hands hold on so strong.

A place for mischief, laughter, and play,
Where the cat pounces on the stray.
We build a fort with pillows and hats,
And hide from the world like clever rats.

Stumbling up, a race we have,
Almost tripping, what a laugh!
Down we careen, it's hard not to grin,
With every stumble, chaos begins.

Through bright days and foggy nights,
These wooden steps hold endless delights.
With giggles and games, we're never short,
Making memories here is always a sport!

Portraits in the Parlor

In the parlor, portraits align,
An awkward bunch with faces divine.
A cousin's grin that's too wide,
Or Auntie's hat, a comical guide.

The wallpaper whispers in old tales,
Of funny faces and misshapen gales.
Furry friends jump in the mix,
Wagging tongues, a humor fix.

You'll find us lounging, tales to share,
As we point and laugh with delight and flair.
Each canvas captures a moment so silly,
While the clock chuckles: "Oh really, oh really?"

With punchlines and quirks, our gatherings glow,
Who needs perfection? The fun's in the show.
In this parlor of laughs, we all belong,
A family portrait, silly and strong!

Solace Among the Beams

Beams above me, wood and charm,
They whisper jokes, keep me from harm.
A spider's dance, a creaky floor,
Each step I take brings laughter more.

The rug's a cloud, where socks go hide,
In cozy corners, giggles slide.
I trip on shoes, they start to laugh,
In silly socks, I take my bath.

Dust bunnies tumble, they're quite the crew,
With every sneeze, they jump anew.
The doorbell rings, it's just the cat,
He winks at me, and that's his chat.

Coffee spills as I reach for snacks,
My house stands tall, it never cracks.
With every mess, I find delight,
In beams and laughs, my heart takes flight.

Sanctuary of Silence

A quiet nook where echoes play,
The fridge hums tunes in a quirky way.
I chase a thought, slip on some cheese,
In this stillness, laughter's easy to seize.

Curtains flutter, they whisper jokes,
While clocks tick softly, in silly strokes.
A chair that wiggles, I'm not alone,
It giggles back, my very own.

Layers of Love

Cozy layers, blankets galore,
They all seem to giggle when I hit the floor.
A snack on my lap, crumbs in my hair,
It's a party here, without a care.

Under cushions, I stash my dreams,
Where nothing's real, or so it seems.
The TV grins with its shiny face,
As I laugh along in a cozy space.

Each drawer a treasure, filled with old jokes,
I find mismatched socks, and cryptic notes.
My house chuckles, a playful friend,
In every corner, the laughter blends.

Embrace of Eaves

Raindrops drumming, a merry beat,
They tap-dance roof till I shuffle my feet.
A squirrel sneaks in for a nibble or two,
I laugh as he flips, what a silly view!

Eaves above, like a grandma's hug,
They wrap me warm when the times get snug.
With each gust of wind, they tell a tale,
Of wacky storms and the postman's pail.

Chairs tell stories, wrinkled and wise,
In polka dots, they catch my sighs.
The cupboard's alive, it giggles at me,
In the home of jests, I'm always free.

Windows to the Soul

Through glassy panes, the world peeks in,
A curious cat with a mischievous grin.
Birds pass by, with a squawk and a flap,
While I sip tea, snug in my comfy lap.

Dust bunnies dance, they twirl and they play,
The curtains flutter like they're part of the fray.
I wave to the neighbors, half dressed in surprise,
Two mismatched socks and a donut for eyes.

The view's quite a show, a comedy spree,
As kids ride their bikes, shouting loudly with glee.
Here I chuckle, in my cozy glass nook,
Watching life unfold like a hilarious book.

A knock at the door, it's the mailman once more,
With parcels of joy and a little galore.
I peek through the window, what a sight to behold,
Hilarity ensues as the story unfolds.

Comfort in the Foundation

Beneath the walls, a bed of jokes lie,
Puns as strong as beams, they never say die.
The floors creak with laughter, all day and night,
Tickling our toes, oh what a delight!

The fridge hums tunes, a silly serenade,
Popcorn pops loudly, like a jolly parade.
In this very place, we dance and we sing,
The foundation holds love, and the joy it can bring.

Under the rug, a surprise or two,
A missing remote, or a shoe that's askew.
With every step, the floors tease and they jest,
Each corner a riot, where giggles are blessed.

So here we reside, in comfort and cheer,
Where every mishap brings a smile near.
This is our haven, and oh what a treat,
In the heart of our home, life's rhythm's so sweet.

Shelter from the Storm

When raindrops tap tap on our sturdy door,
We cozy up tight, who could want more?
The thunder's a drummer, the lightning a show,
While we hid inside, warm with snacks in tow.

Pillow forts rise like castles of dreams,
Where giggles erupt and laughter just beams.
With chips as our armor, we brave the wet fray,
Each crunch whispers tales of our sly, fun play.

Outside, it's a downpour, a monsoon of gray,
But inside our refuge, we all shout hooray!
The sky might be grumpy, but here all's just right,
Adventures abound on this stormy delight.

So we watch all the rain through our windows of glee,
As we dance in our socks, two left feet full of spree.
In our fortress of fun, we reduce life to play,
Finding joy in the tempest, come what may!

Radiance in the Hall

In the hall, there's a glow from the lamps on the wall,
Each bulb a spotlight, ready for all.
With pictures that giggle, from moments long past,
Every frame tells a joke, though some are a blast!

Here walks the cat, a royal parade,
With a strut like a king, he won't be dismayed.
A mirror reflects all, in the most funny ways,
As it captures our smiles, on our silliest days.

The coat rack's alive, a stoic dear friend,
Holding hats, coats, and laughter that never will end.
With a wink and a nod, it shares in our cheer,
As we tumble and dance, bringing joy ever near.

So linger in the hall, let the laughter unwind,
With stories and giggles that life has designed.
In this radiant space, where joy's freely found,
Let the echoes of laughter forever rebound.

Serenade of Serenity

Within these walls, I hide away,
My socks clash bright, it's laundry day.
The fridge hums tunes of bygone snacks,
I dance with spills as no one lacks.

A pet cat judges every move,
Caught mid-air on a cheese fondue.
The couch sighs loud, it knows my weight,
A throne of crumbs, a nesting fate.

The clock ticks slowly, I sip my tea,
Imagining adventures, wild and free.
But here I laugh and snuggle tight,
This goofy life feels just so right.

So raise a glass to joyous mess,
In cozy chaos, I find my bless.
For home's the stage of silly plays,
Where laughter echoes through my days.

Timeless Embrace

Under this roof, the roof of dreams,
I trip on toys, or so it seems.
The ceiling's cracked with stories told,
Of every laugh, and every bold.

The fridge's light, a shining sun,
A midnight snack, oh what a run!
I swear the walls could burst with cheer,
As quirky steps draw friends near.

A laundry basket, my secret chair,
I nod in sleep, without a care.
Dreaming of worlds where I am king,
In wrinkled crowns, I reign supreme.

With parents' jokes that never fade,
And siblings' pranks that I've displayed.
A tapestry of life unfolds,
In messy corners, the heart holds.

The Heart of Living

Here in my nook, I thrive and play,
With mismatched socks, the fashion sway.
My cat's disapproval, a daily show,
As I strut in my lovably low.

The coffee spills, a tragic dance,
I laugh it off, give chaos a chance.
Inknocking on walls, the echoes sing,
Of epic battles, where I'm the king.

My kitchen's a labyrinth of pizza crust,
A culinary art forged in rush.
With every bite, joy's recipe,
In every crumb, life's jubilee.

So here's to comfort, to snacks galore,
With giggles and hugs, who could ask for more?
This may be madness, but oh, it's mine,
In this crazy heart, I happily dine.

Back to Where It Began

I return to the place of silly schemes,
Where every corner holds vibrant dreams.
The rug's a stage for my dance routines,
And the walls, plot twists, in crazy scenes.

The old rocking chair creaks with pride,
As I skateboard past, in joyful stride.
My dog's the audience, tail wagging fast,
For each goofy tumble, my legendary cast.

In the kitchen, scents of burnt delight,
Mom's gourmet fails in plain sight.
As laughter bubbles over the stove,
In this charred chaos, I find my grove.

And so, like a sitcom, this life unfolds,
With hugs and humor that never grows old.
I'll rest my head in this beloved nest,
In this joyful circus, I am truly blessed.

The Comfort Between Four Walls

Within these walls, I find my glee,
A couch that hugs to set me free.
The fridge hums tunes, it's quite the show,
Where leftovers dance in a row.

The cat steals naps while I just stare,
At dishes piled, a mountain there.
No need for fancy, grand decor,
Just chaos wrapped in love galore.

Heartstrings of a Dwelling

Houses speak in creaks and sighs,
A symphony of lows and highs.
The bathroom's always on a quest,
For peace when nature's at its best.

In corners lie forgotten socks,
Like treasures from old, ticklish clocks.
The laundry pile, a mountain high,
That greets me with a knowing sigh.

Pillars of Peace

Four sturdy walls and a roof so bright,
Where whispered secrets take flight.
My kitchen's a laboratory mad,
Where burnt toast can unexpectedly be bad.

Pillows like clouds, all cuddly and thick,
Playing tag with a wayward stick.
The coffee maker hums a tune,
As sunlight spills like a happy boon.

Echoes of Laughter

Echoes bounce off the cheerful walls,
Where laughter leads and chaos calls.
Family feuds over board games sway,
As rules are bent in a playful way.

Tickling toes and silly pranks,
Filling echoing spaces with thanks.
Each room a joke, each laugh a thread,
In this happy maze where joy is spread.

Beneath the Roof

In the snug corner, the cat lies flat,
With a fishing pole made from a spatula.
The dog chases shadows, oh what a sight,
Never quite sure if it's day or night.

Socks on the ceiling fan spin like a dream,
Mom says it's dust, but we call it cream.
Laughing so hard, we fall on the floor,
Wondering how there could be so much more.

Beneath this covering, life is a game,
A cozy arena where no one's to blame.
Tickling the belly of time with a grin,
It's all in the quirks, where laughter begins.

Dinner's a mystery—what will we snack?
Mismatched leftovers piled in a stack.
Together we feast, on whatever we find,
Who knew a brown blob could be so refined?

Memories in Every Room

In the kitchen, spills tell tales of the night,
Pasta on the ceiling, a peculiar sight.
Grandma's old spatula still holds a grin,
It wobbles and dances, let the chaos begin.

The living room cushions, once plump and neat,
Now hold the secrets of snack time defeat.
Whispers of laughter and echoes of games,
A stage for the antics of wild, silly names.

Upstairs in the hall, are ghosts of my shoes,
Slippers that scamper, like errant little mu's.
They lead down the hallway with curious haste,
Chasing the echoes of cake I won't waste.

In every room, there's a laugh to be had,
Even the bathroom can't help but feel glad.
With bubbles and slip-ups, it's all in a whirl,
Memories caught in a playful twirl.

Archways of Affection

Under the arch where the dust bunnies play,
Lurking beneath all the toys in dismay.
A battle of laughter and a fortress of shoes,
Each corner holds tales, oh, who can refuse?

The dining room table, a battlefield feast,
Where broccoli monsters make children cease.
We giggle and wiggle, dodging the greens,
In this whimsical world, nothing's as it seems.

Each archway a window to memories we find,
Crammed in the spaces where love intertwines.
We dance down the hall with our socks on our hands,
In this funhouse of laughter, the silliness stands.

Come join our parade through the rooms we adore,
A carnival spirit lives forevermore.
With echoes of joy that steep into dreams,
Life's just a jolly ride bursting at seams!

Guardian of Solitude

There's a corner in the quiet, where the chair goes to nap,
Draped in old blankets, like a comfy little trap.
The dust bunnies gather, plotting their schemes,
Shhh! Don't wake the guardian—keep mumbling dreams.

Pillows stacked high and a blanket fort strong,
Where superheroes gather but never belong.
With a giggle and whisper, we share our big plans,
Conquer the universe with just our bare hands!

The bathroom's a fortress with walls made of tiles,
Echoing laughter for what feels like miles.
The guardian shushes, "This is our zone!"
In the bubble of warmth, we're never alone.

Down in the cellar, old treasures we glimpse,
Mismatched jars filled with candy and hints.
Here sits the guardian, arms crossed and wise,
A keeper of secrets and playful surprise.

The Space Between Us

In my room, I hear a sneeze,
A ghost? No, just my cat at ease.
The laundry's piled high like a hill,
Yet somehow, silence holds a thrill.

The fridge hums tunes of takeout bliss,
While socks perform a sock puppet kiss.
The couch is where lost keys reside,
And crumbs, oh crumbs, our nightly guide.

Sunlit Memories and Shadows.

Sunbeams dance on floors of dust,
Chasing shadows, a silly must.
I trip on toys left in a heap,
In this playhouse, we laugh and leap.

The kitchen's always got a smell,
Of burnt toast—dinner went to hell.
Yet in the chaos, joy's a friend,
In every mess, the fun won't end.

Haven in the Walls

Walls hold secrets, tales of grace,
Yet also, where I lost the race.
That one time, fell down the stairs,
Oops! Hope no one really cares.

Nooks hide treasures, dusty shrouds,
Like snacks tucked in, our laughter loud.
In every corner, giggles nest,
A home feels silly, but it's the best.

Embrace of Four Corners

Four corners hold our little quirks,
Like mismatched socks and silly smirks.
The ceiling fan spins like a pro,
While we sing off-key in a show.

A couch that swallows, worn and wide,
Where snacks and stories both reside.
Each creak and groan brings us closer,
In this home, forget the toaster!

Nook of Serenity

In a corner where dust bunnies play,
My socks partner up for a ballet.
Chairs that creak with a whimsical tune,
Spilling secrets beneath the full moon.

Laundry piles like mountains so high,
I'm convinced they're plotting to fly.
Yet laughter echoes within these walls,
As I dodge my dog and his tennis ball.

Mismatched curtains, a sight to behold,
With stories untold, that never grow old.
The fridge hums a lullaby, it seems,
Cooking up chaos with baked potato dreams.

So here I'll lounge, let the world spin,
In this house, my joys begin.
With quirky moments, piles of delight,
My cozy nook, a source of light.

Tapestry of Togetherness

We gather 'round for a feast of odd,
With burnt toast and a very stern nod.
The cat's on the counter, the dog at my feet,
In this mix of chaos, nothing can beat.

Sibling rivalry makes quite the show,
Over who controls the TV remote flow.
But with laughter spilling like pasta from pots,
Together we are, in all our crazy knots.

Leftover pizza finds its way in,
While I search for snacks, at a winsome grin.
Each story shared is a bond we weave,
In our fabric of memories, we never leave.

So toast to the mayhem, the joy, the mess,
In this tapestry, I truly am blessed.
With each silly moment, taken to heart,
Together forever, we'll never part.

A Place to Belong

Found here amidst rubber bands and pens,
Where time sometimes stops and never ends.
My chair has a dip from all the long reads,
Waiting for wisdom to plant some new seeds.

The fridge is a puzzle of mismatched delight,
Leftovers dance like they own the night.
Sticky notes sprout on the table in rows,
Reminders of what nobody knows.

A treasure chest filled with socks and old ties,
And a pet goldfish who flirts with the flies.
Here's where I land when the world gets tough,
In my quirky kingdom, the love is enough.

So here's to the laughter, the joy, and the song,
In this cherished domain where I truly belong.
With giggles and comfort, all snug and tight,
This whimsical spot is my heart's delight.

Memories Tucked in Corners

Amidst cobwebs and a box of old shoes,
Lies the evidence of laughter and blues.
Jokes on the walls, peeling paint with flair,
Each scratch tells a story; come sit, if you dare.

Forgotten toys whisper tales from the past,
As the clock ticks rhythm, it's never too fast.
The dog snores comfortably on the old rug,
While I search for clues with a curious shrug.

A vase full of memories, slightly askew,
It holds all the moments, both silly and true.
With echoes of laughter and whispers of care,
In these quaint corners, my heart's in the air.

So let me wander, where the shadows blend,
In this quirky haven, I make and I mend.
With joy packed away in every little nook,
I find my peace with the tales that it took.

Loving the Imperfect

A creaky floor sings its own song,
Dancing with every step, it can't be wrong.
A fridge that hums more than it chills,
Uninvited guests? Just the house's thrills.

Dust bunnies have their own little dance,
Hosting parties when I'm not in a trance.
Walls with sketches of love and cheer,
Imperfect art, but it's what we hold dear.

The cracks in the wall, a tale to unfold,
Of laughter and mishaps that never get old.
The paint that's peeling, they say it's a sign,
Just adds to the charm, makes it divine.

So here's to the quirks, let's laugh and cheer,
For the beauty of life is found right here.
In every odd corner that we adore,
Loving the imperfect, who could ask for more?

The Space Between Us

In this cozy nook where we both reside,
Cushion forts built with endless pride.
Remote controls staged in a mighty fight,
Navigating through chaos, oh what a sight!

Dinner's a mystery, what's in that pot?
Spaghetti or mystery? Let's take a shot!
The microwave beeps like a clock gone mad,
We share a grin and the leftover fad.

When socks take a leap, it's a curious fate,
Where do they vanish? We ponder and wait.
Each missing pair tells a tale to embrace,
The laughter we share fills our sacred space.

In the space between us, a love so wide,
Made of silly moments, we take in our stride.
Laughter a thread that binds us so tight,
In our little haven, it all feels right.

Roof of Resilience

The roof may sag, but it holds its ground,
Like a stubborn cat, refusing to be found.
Raindrops tapping in a rhythmic tick,
Nature's little drummer with a perfect trick.

It's patched with memories both old and new,
A splash of paint, a sunbeam breakthrough.
Each groove tells tales of storms once fought,
A triumph of laughter, the lessons we sought.

The kitchen's aroma, a feast for the soul,
With burnt toast and coffee, we feel so whole.
Under this rooftop, we dance through the night,
Finding joy in the chaos, everything feels right.

Though tiles may slip and the rafters creak,
Our laughter echoes, growing stronger each week.
In this haphazard place where we play and dream,
The roof of resilience, it shines and beams.

Forgotten Corners of Joy

In the nooks where the sunlight rarely creeps,
Lies a stuffed bear guard that silently keeps.
Forgotten corners with treasures in sight,
Each finds a story, each treasure ignites.

A long-lost sock and a misplaced shoe,
Together they form a legendary crew.
Whispers of laughter linger on the stair,
Echoes of memories twirl in the air.

Dust dances gently, a slow ballet,
In forgotten spaces where dreams like to play.
Behind old curtains, new worlds arise,
The quirky oddities become the best prize.

So cherish the corners where joy likes to hide,
In the chaos of life, let wonder abide.
For in the forgotten, life truly begins,
A treasure of laughter, our greatest wins.

Dreams Under the Eaves

When I sneak to bed, my socks in a heap,
Napping away, with secrets to keep.
A mouse scurries by, in a tuxedo so fine,
Eating my cheddar, oh how divine!

The walls start to giggle, the floorboards sway,
Whispering tales of the silliest play.
A cat on a mission, with dreams in its head,
Plotting to catch that mouse in my bed!

Fables of the Hearth

The stove's got a story, a bubbling tale,
Of soup that went swimming and never found sail.
Dad claims the spatula waltzes at night,
While we laugh and we dance by the soft candlelight.

The bread has a burp that echoes so loud,
As the oven takes pride like a king in a crowd.
Each meal a new fable, both wacky and wild,
With flavors and quips that would make grandma smile.

An Invitation to Belong

The couch has seen laughter, some pillows in tears,
As friends gather 'round to swap all their fears.
A blanket fort castle we proudly declare,
With a moat made of snacks in our little lair.

The door creaks and chuckles, it knows all our names,
The echoes that bounce tell our wildest games.
So come one, come all, to our goofy retreat,
Where laughter's the language and joy's on repeat.

Windows of Possibility

Peeking through windows, my neighbors are bright,
One's urging a cat to perform in the night.
Another's concocting a pasta delight,
While the dog on a leash pulls for a quick bite.

A bird on the ledge starts a chorus so sweet,
Singing of wishes and whimsical feet.
With each little glance, a new story unfolds,
In the house with the curtains, where laughter is gold.

Light Filtering Through the Glass

Sunbeams dance on floors, they play,
Dust bunnies join the bright ballet.
Rain streaks laughter down the pane,
Windows giggle in the rain.

Curtains sway like whispers sweet,
A breeze brings tickles to your feet.
Mismatched socks in sunlight gleam,
A wacky family's silly dream.

Foundation of Love

Bricks laid down with laughter loud,
Echoes of joy beneath the shroud.
Nuts and bolts of silly fights,
Patchwork hearts on starry nights.

Under this roof, quirks align,
Wobbly dances, and jello's fine.
Foundations built on hugs and cheer,
Cemented in the laughter near.

The Waiting Arms of Home

Doors swing wide with open arms,
Welcomes bloom with quirky charms.
Shoes piled high, a comical scene,
Who knew such chaos could be keen?

In every nook, a memory spun,
Mismatched spoons for gumdrop fun.
Mirrors reflect our zany ways,
Home's a circus that joyfully stays.

Frames of Forgiveness

Picture frames with smiles galore,
Captured moments, riotous lore.
Artistic fights, a canvas wide,
Stains of laughter, tear, then glide.

Snapshots of blunders that we make,
Wacky faces, a silly shake.
In these frames, our love grows bright,
Forgiveness wrapped in quirky light.

Shelter from the Whirlwind

When winds blow wild and rain does dance,
Inside I chuckle, take a chance.
The roof's my shield, my happy dome,
Here in my chaos, I feel at home.

The neighbors peek, their eyes go wide,
As I juggle muffins, tossed with pride.
A flying cake? Oh what a feat!
My kitchen's a circus, but can't be beat!

My cat's a guard, with whiskers keen,
He chases shadows, thinks he's a queen.
Together we laugh, we sip our tea,
In this tornado of glee, just him and me.

So if you seek a place of cheer,
Join my delightful, whirling sphere.
With laughter loud, and snacks to share,
You'll find your joy, if you just dare!

A Place to Rest the Heart

In every corner, laughter lies,
With socks and shoes in strange disguise.
The couch has seen so many naps,
A kingdom built of cozy traps.

The fridge hums tunes, a friend, so dear,
With leftovers laughing, "Eat us here!"
Each snack a tale of last night's thrill,
Voices echo, time stands still.

The plants have names, yes, every one,
We have debates on who's more fun.
With pots and pans, I dance all night,
A funny sight, what a delight!

So here I dwell, in joyful mess,
A noisy home, no need to stress.
With every quirk, I take my part,
In this peculiar, merry heart.

Homestead of Solace

With creaky floors that squeak and croak,
My homestead whispers secret jokes.
Where socks go missing, and forks conspire,
To start a party in the fire!

The walls adorned with pictures won,
Of family feuds and half-fun runs.
A coffee stain becomes a star,
In this gallery of who we are.

The dog thinks he's the ruler here,
With tiny paws, he holds no fear.
He flips and rolls, a furry ball,
In laughter's arms, we have it all.

So bring your quirks, your funny ways,
In this merry home where chaos plays.
We'll bake a mess, drink tales untold,
In this sweet haven, hearts unfold.

Guardians of the Threshold

At the door, two cats, quite stout,
Stand as guards, with a judgy pout.
They eye the guests with regal flair,
Will you pass, or is it a dare?

With muddy shoes and giggles loud,
They wonder just who's in their crowd.
They plot the best spots on the rug,
To steal the warmth, oh how they hug!

With coats and hats tossed on the floor,
We laugh and chatter, more and more.
The threshold's lined with silly tales,
Of lost umbrellas, and goofy flails.

So welcome in, let laughter swell,
In this realm where stories dwell.
With guardians fierce, and hearts so free,
We'll craft a world of hilarity!

Sanctuary of Shadows

In the corners, dust bunnies sit,
Whispering tales, oh what a bit!
Couch potato kingdom, we reign supreme,
Silent groans echo, not quite a dream.

Fridge raids at midnight, what a delight,
Leftover pizza, a marvelous sight!
Socks as décor, mismatched and free,
Who needs fashion? Just me and my spree!

Under blankets, we play hide and seek,
Chasing the cat, oh what a cheek!
Laughter erupts like a soda can,
In our little castle, we're a wild clan.

Windows crack open for a breeze to fight,
Here's to our fortress, our goofy light!
Walls damp with stories, secrets we share,
A home full of chaos, but we don't care!

Nestled Dreams

In our nests of cushions, we laugh till we cry,
With a pizza slice high, we reach for the sky!
Neighbors might wonder what's wrong with our crew,
But they'll never quite guess just how much we chew.

Down the hallway, giggles abound,
Spilling the secrets that we've tightly bound.
A family of quirkies, all snug as a bug,
Hiding from chores, with a mischievous shrug.

Painted walls hold secrets we'd never release,
Like the time Grandpa danced dressed up like a beast.
With every mischief, our love only grows,
In this goofy domain, anything goes!

The ceiling fan spins, a whirlwind of grace,
Collecting our laughter, what a wild race!
Nestled together, our dreams take flight,
In this silly home, every day is just right!

Homeward Bound Memories

Socks on the ceiling, a curious sight,
Home's a wild place where we reign at night.
Pizza boxes courtesy of our feast,
Grumbling about chores? We're really the least!

Mom's hidden stash, the good snacks galore,
A treasure hunt mission right down to the core.
Sneaky little giggles in the pantry store,
Who knew being naughty could open such doors?

The dog snores loudly, a symphony grand,
While we plot our next con, all perfectly planned.
A fortress of laughter, both silly and sweet,
In this quirky abode, life feels complete!

Fuzzy blankets piled up high like a hill,
To stay cozy and warm, we've mastered the skill.
With memories made, we all laugh out loud,
In our whimsical palace, we cheerfully crowd!

Cradle of Comfort

In the heart of this laughter, we gather each noon,
With chips in our hands and a silly balloon.
Under the table, the dog steals the show,
While cheese spells giggles—who needs a pro?

Whirling fans cradle our wildest of dreams,
While we plot on the couch, or so it seems.
Socks everywhere, a fashion of sorts,
Who said mismatched was just for the ports?

Walls echo stories of pranks and of cheers,
Inside joke moments dusted with tears.
We turn up the tunes, dancing like mad,
In this cradle we've built, we're happily glad!

As the sunsets color our windows aglow,
We gather 'round tales of the way things would go.
With laughter and snacks in this cozy delight,
Our hearts are all full, what a glorious night!

Hearthside Whispers

A cat sprawled, blocking the heat,
An oven's laughter, work is sweet.
Mismatched socks dance near the flame,
In this circus, who's to blame?

Cushions leap with words unsaid,
The dog is king, and he's well-fed.
Pizza rolls on plates amassed,
In our own world, we're unsurpassed!

The fridge hums tunes of midnight snack,
As feet find floor, and the toast goes back.
In jokey jibes, we find our glee,
Under this roof, it's wild and free!

When laughter ricochets off the walls,
We dance like dorks in the empty halls.
And though it's crazy, we wouldn't trade,
For these merry moments, our love we've made.

Walls That Hold Us

A paint of yellow drips in glee,
As kids make art of the TV.
Pasta launches, a noodle fight,
Squabbles paint the walls, what a sight!

The doorbell rings, a pizza guy,
We tip with slices, oh me, oh my!
Furries scamper, chase their tails,
As laughter fills our silly trails!

Stickers scatter on the floor,
A treasure hunt in every drawer.
Press pause on chaos, take a nap,
Life inside here's a cozy trap.

Echoes of giggles in every nook,
Hiding secrets, come take a look.
Time bends here in this friendly mess,
In these walls, we find our best.

Safety Beyond the Door

Shoelaces tangled, wide open shoes,
Sock puppets sing the most silly blues.
Lost in the thrill of hide and seek,
The corners whisper, secrets they keep.

The mailbox grins with junk inside,
While flavors grace the refrigerator's ride.
Messy tables, adventures galore,
Turn the mundane to a great encore!

Chase the dust bunnies, don't be shy,
Under the couch, they hide and lie.
Pillow forts built, rebellion is here,
With just a wink and a joyous cheer.

Knock-knock jokes echo past the pane,
And on this floor, we'll dance in the rain.
Beyond the door lies the world so grand,
But in here, we're in our wonderland!

Refuge in the Frame

Framed photos grin, hearts on display,
As socks decide to have a play.
The coffee pot brews laughter and cheer,
In this goofy haven, there's nothing to fear!

Glimmers of light through dusty panes,
Silly dances in colorful chains.
A dog in sunglasses lounges with flair,
This is the place where we simply don't care!

Tangled in blankets, lost in a book,
The cat claims the seat with a regal look.
Spoons become instruments, dinner's a show,
In this frame of ours, love's all we know.

So buckle your seatbelts, here we go,
With laughter and warmth, we steal the show.
In this wild laughter, we find our grace,
This quirky refuge is our happy place.

Where Memories Reside

In the corner, a cat snores loud,
As kids spill juice, oh how they're proud!
The couch is stained from snacks galore,
Yet love grows here, forevermore.

Old shoes still dance, where dust bunnies play,
While laughter echoes through the day.
Each wall holds secrets, come hear their tales,
In this kingdom of comfort, joy never fails.

A Tapestry of Togetherness

Grandma's hat on a chair, hat askew,
As grandpa claims he once flew!
Their laughter bursts, a bubbly tune,
While socks hide out, like little raccoons.

The kitchen sings of burnt toast fights,
And mysteries of baking, oh what delights!
Silly stories shared over tea,
In this patchwork, we're wild and free.

The Safe Abode

With the ceiling fan spinning like a top,
And socks mixed up? Oh, fun never stops!
We play hide and seek, who's under the bed?
Oh, it's just the dog! Where's my head?

The smell of popcorn, movies on cue,
With pillows tossed, we create our zoo.
In this space, chaos is a friend,
Where joy and laughter never end.

Dreams Woven in Corners

Under the stairs, where dreams like to creep,
A mountain of laundry, a monster so steep.
Pajamas hang out in a tangle of glee,
Whispering secrets, just between me.

The front door squeaks, a melody sweet,
As we gather 'round for our nightly treat.
With stories spun and giggles that soar,
In this whimsical place, who could ask for more?

Haven Beneath the Roof

In a house of quirks and squeaky stairs,
Cats rule the roost with their silly stares.
Noisy neighbors hoot like owls at night,
We laugh at the chaos, it brings pure delight.

The fridge hums tunes like a jazz café,
And socks hide out in a secret ballet.
Pants and shirts dance in a laundry swirl,
This wacky abode makes my head twirl.

Mystery stains on the kitchen floor,
A relic of snacks we can't ignore.
Crumbs are our confetti, left in a trail,
In this playful haven, we'll never fail.

Guests arrive, and the chaos expands,
We serve snacks from our mismatched hands.
Every corner a tale, laughter in the air,
In this amusing space, we have naught a care.

Walls that Whisper Warmth

These walls, they talk, with each creak and groan,
Sharing old secrets, a legend of stone.
With each loud thud of a careless feet,
A rhyming ruckus, no one can beat.

Dinner conversations are loud and bright,
Forks in a duel, oh what a sight!
'Pass the potatoes!' we holler with glee,
While we trip over chairs like a comical spree.

Here's where the cat plays hopscotch with pride,
The dog barks rhythms, our own house wide.
It's more like a circus, no doubt it's true,
With laughter our currency, we bid adieu.

Under the roof, we're a quirky clan,
Dreams as wild as the whirly-whirl fan.
No need for perfection, just good-hearted fun,
In our slanted house, we have already won.

Embrace of Timber and Stone

With wooden beams that sway and bend,
This home's a party that never does end.
The floors groove to music we can't hear,
While socks throw themselves with unpredictable cheer.

The kitchen is where mischief brews,
Baking blunders turn to comic views.
Flour clouds burst like a snowy parade,
And laughter erupts in a cavalcade.

Fortress of fun, where dreams collide,
Doorways of laughter, nothing to hide.
Here every blunder is simply a jest,
Creating a memory, we always invest.

Nooks filled with treasures from days gone by,
Each dust bunny a friend that waves goodbye.
Our quirky domicile, a whimsical scheme,
In the haven we've crafted, we live our dream.

Hearthbeat of Home

In our cozy abode where the laughter's alive,
Furniture dances, it seems to thrive.
Chairs gossip softly, tables have tales,
While the coffee pot hums like a ship with sails.

Socks on the floor, a mismatched brigade,
Lost in the chaos, our own charade.
The cat on the rug, a self-proclaimed king,
Draped like a blanket, he owns everything.

Slightly askew, the pictures they hang,
Each frame a story of laughter and clang.
Here quirks are cherished, ridiculous and grand,
With every zany moment, love takes the stand.

So raise up your mugs to the wit of our den,
To the humor that spirals, again and again.
We gather our stories, with smiles we hone,
In the heart of our happiness, we call it home.

Refuge from the Storm

Raindrops patter on the sheet,
Inside, we're dancing to the beat.
A pot of soup upon the stove,
We laugh as bubbles start to rove.

The cat's asleep atop a chair,
While we debate who's done the hair.
Checking leaks with giddy glee,
This house is where we're meant to be.

With every creak, we make a sound,
A game of hide-and-seek around.
The thunder claps, a wild song,
But here, we feel we do belong.

So while the tempest starts to roar,
We're cheerful as we hear it pour.
A fort of cushions, thick and deep,
In laughter's arms, we drift to sleep.

Nestled in Familiarity

In corners where the laughter bounces,
With mismatched chairs and funny flounces.
Our socks are scattered, what a sight,
Yet here we find our hearts' delight.

Outdated jokes on walls adorned,
The kitchen's always slightly scorned.
But every crack and every care,
Is woven love, so rare and fair.

The floorboards creak like olden tales,
Where every step unlocks the gales.
We giggle at the quirky sound,
In this, our home, pure joy is found.

Through messy rooms and bright mishaps,
Nestled tight in all our gaps.
With every moment, warmth remains,
In cozy chaos, love sustains.

Sanctuary in Shadows

In corners dark, the secrets creep,
While shifty shadows sing and peep.
Cushions piled high like mountain tops,
In silly forts, our laughter hops.

The TV's always blaring loud,
Yet we embrace our little crowd.
In tangled lights and whispered schemes,
Our homes become the sweetest dreams.

The evening brings a playful scare,
With ghostly tales and fun to share.
As twilight flickers, hearts get bold,
In this warm space, our tales unfold.

While every night's a thrill and chase,
We find our joys in every place.
This playful haunt, our hearts will dwell,
Within these walls, all is quite well.

Windows to the Soul

Through panes of glass, the world does peep,
With all its noise, it makes us leap.
Yet here inside, we're snug and warm,
In jolly banter, we transform.

The view outside, a frantic dance,
While we engage in silly prance.
Each window mocks with fog and frost,
Yet in our laughter, time is lost.

The flowers bloom, the curtains sway,
As we set forth on our wild play.
With funny faces to the glass,
We wave goodbye to all that's crass.

Our giddy hearts, like kites they soar,
As we embrace the fun galore.
These windows, oh, they frame our cheer,
In every glance, our joy draws near.

Hearthstone Reflections

At times it creaks, this wooden floor,
Dancing dust bunnies tumble more.
The cat has claimed the best sun spot,
While I hunt snacks — maybe I'm not hot.

The couch, it swallows me whole each night,
Joined by snacks that sneak out of sight.
Remote control wars, who gets to steer?
Laughing when I 'lose' — I can't even hear!

The fridge hums symphonies of delight,
Ice cubes rattle, a cool paradise bite.
I ponder life with a pickle in hand,
This mighty fortress covers all, quite grand!

Windows creak, with whispers of breeze,
Tales of neighbors — oh, if you please!
Here we gather, giggles on the scene,
In my silly realm, it's all quite serene.

Echoes in the Entryway

Each time I trip over my own two feet,
The shoes at the door laugh, oh what a feat!
I stumble in with bags piled high,
And wonder how they multiply — oh my!

Sticky fingerprints greet me each day,
Tales of little ones, messily at play.
Walls adorned with scribbles and cheer,
Home's a gallery of giggles, oh dear!

Dinner's a saga of burnt and charred,
Followed by tales of the nosy yard.
Neighbors peering, what's going amiss?
A burnt casserole — not some gourmet bliss!

Yet laughter bounces off each wall,
In this quirky labyrinth, I gladly fall.
For every slip, and spill, and mess,
Echoes of joy, I must confess.

Threshold of Warmth

Upon the mat, socks stray and roam,
While my trusty slippers reclaim their home.
Visitors state, 'How cozy it feels!',
Avoiding our chaos like it's made of meals.

In the kitchen, wild smells drift and dance,
Food in the pot gives me my chance.
"Dinner's ready!" becomes quite the show,
It's takeout again—this I readily know!

Chairs piled high with a mountain of clothes,
Playful debates over 'who's next to do those'.
The pets all snicker, knowing their tasks,
While we bicker about the roles that it masks.

Yet every night as the moon begins to rise,
We settle down, with laughter that flies.
For within all the clutter and games we partake,
Lies a warmth of love that none can forsake.

Pillars of Peace

Cupboards creak as I search for a snack,
Navigating chaos, I've got no knack.
The sound of giggles from another room,
Diving into laundry, they'll need a vacuum!

Silly motifs line the hall's bright walls,
Family portraits in hilarious sprawls.
Every glance triggers a hearty grin,
Memories gathered, where laughter begins.

The bathroom battles — who's hogging the sink?
Shampoo wars rage while the kitchen dinks.
But as the night settles, chairs start to sway,
Inside this haven, we find our way.

In moments of madness, we truly see,
Love blooms within this whimsical spree.
Footprints of joy traced all around,
In the pillars of laughter, we're forever bound.

In the Lap of Time

Couches sag in all the right ways,
Where socks fight for space, it stays.
The fridge hums off-key, a choir's tune,
While leftovers plot their next balloon.

Walls witness my dance to the fridge,
Sporting my PJs, I'm a grand midge.
Tick-tock's the beat of our zany steps,
As dust bunnies play chess with our pets.

Honey, did you find that shirt? No way!
It looks like a cat made it go astray.
In here, fashion's a ruffled dream,
Matching socks? Just not my theme!

With the remote always lost, that's real art,
In the lap of time, it beats with heart.
Each wall holds a memory, cheerfully crooked,
Home's just a circus, joyfully hooked.

Foundation of Dreams

In the basement, our secrets do thrive,
Where old bikes and memories jive.
A foundation built with giggles and grunts,
And echoes of 'Where are the stunts?'

Nails and screws, our instruments rare,
Fixing toys can lead to despair.
Yet each hammer hit sings a new song,
As laughter builds, we can't go wrong.

A pot that leaks, we plant a dread,
While dad's quick fixes run away instead.
But in each flaw, find dreams galore,
A house that's not dull, who could ask for more?

With blueprints drawn in crayon red,
Imagination feeds our everyday bread.
In this dwelling, we thrive in schemes,
Building castles from whimsical dreams.

Scents of Home

Brownies baked with a side of whoopee,
While dad's burnt toast has room for a boogie.
The kitchen sings with spices and glee,
As cats dive into flour like it's a spree.

That scent of chaos, love in the air,
Where each meal's a gamble, a whimsical dare.
The fridge is a graveyard of half-eaten pies,
With sticky note secrets, oh what a surprise!

Mom's perfume swirls into the day,
Mixing with toothpaste, 'It's coming your way!'
Each corner carries a story to share,
Filled with chuckles, and love everywhere.

So here's to the odors of life and its charm,
A recipe for joy, a sprinkle of calm.
In this fabulous mix, we always rehearse,
Making the mundane forever diverse.

Echoes of Laughter

Under the roof, where silliness flows,
Echoes of giggles, everything glows.
The hallway sings with whispers of cheer,
We chase moonbeams as bedtime draws near.

In the shadows, hide-and-seek's bold,
A journey through corners, young hearts unfold.
With every tickle, a squeal so bright,
Memories dance in the soft twilight.

The living room's chaos, a magical mess,
Pillows turned forts, we aim to impress.
Though crumbs scatter, ambitions still soar,
In this fortress of joy, we're never a bore.

So let the laughter break down the walls,
In every hiccup, our spirit enthralls.
Through echoes of fun, we continue to play,
In the heart of our haven, we seize the day.